WITHDRAWN

GRAPHIC DINOSAURS

DIPLODOCUS

THE WHIP-TAILED DINOSAUR

ILLUSTRATED BY JAMES FIELD

PowerKiDS
press

New York

Published in 2009 by The Rosen Publishing Group, Inc.
29 East 21st Street, New York, NY 10010

Copyright © 2009 David West Books

All rights reserved. No part of this book may be reproduced in any form without permission in writing from the publisher, except by a reviewer.

Designed and produced by
David West Books

Designed and written by Rob Shone
Editor: Ronne Randall
Consultant: Steve Parker, Senior Scientific Fellow, Zoological Society of London
Photographic credits: 5t, Quadell; 5m, Ballista; 30, istockphoto.com/Sam Lee.

Library of Congress Cataloging-in-Publication Data

Shone, Rob.
Diplodocus : the whip-tailed dinosaur / Rob Shone.
p. cm. — (Graphic dinosaurs)
Includes index.
ISBN 978-1-4358-2504-8 (library binding)
ISBN 978-1-4042-7714-4 (pbk.)
ISBN 978-1-4042-7718-2 (6-pack)
1. Diplodocus—Juvenile literature. I. Title.
QE862.S3S445 2009
567.913—dc22

2008003924

Manufactured in China

CONTENTS

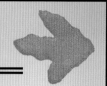

WHAT IS A DIPLODOCUS?

DIPLODOCUS MEANS "DOUBLE BEAM"

➤ *Diplodocus backbones were hollow. This meant the dinosaur weighed less than it could have.*

➤ *Diplodocus's tail was long, and its end was very thin. Scientists think that it could have been cracked like a whip to scare enemies away.*

➤ *Diplodocus could not chew its food. Instead, it swallowed stones, called gastroliths, to grind up food in its stomach.*

➤ *Diplodocus's brain was small, about as big as a man's fist.*

➤ *Fossilized skin marks show that Diplodocus had spines running along its back as some modern-day lizards do.*

➤ *Diplodocus teeth were shaped like pencils. The Diplodocuses only had teeth at the front of their mouths.*

➤ *Diplodocus had a claw on the first toe of each front foot. It might have used its claws to defend itself against enemies.*

DIPLODOCUS WAS A DINOSAUR THAT LIVED AROUND 145 MILLION TO 155 MILLION YEARS AGO, DURING THE JURASSIC PERIOD. FOSSILS OF ITS SKELETON HAVE BEEN FOUND IN NORTH AMERICA.

 An adult Diplodocus measured up to 90 feet (27 m) long, and weighed up to 17.5 tons (15,876 kg).

HEADS...

For such a large animal, Diplodocus's head was small. Its neck grew up to 20 feet (6 m) long, but it could not lift its head much higher than its back. Diplodocus likely spent most of its time eating ferns and young trees that grew near the ground. Along the hollow bones of its neck were air sacs. They were connected to its lungs and could be blown up like balloons. They helped keep the neck straight and stiff.

The large holes in Diplodocus's skull made it very light.

...AND TAILS

Diplodocus had a very long tail made up of over 80 bones. It gets its name, "Double Beam," from the bones that lie on the underside of its tail. These bones (also called chevrons) are found in pairs and look like roof beams. Scientists think the chevrons helped Diplodocus stand on its back legs. The chevrons protected the tail as it propped up the dinosaur.

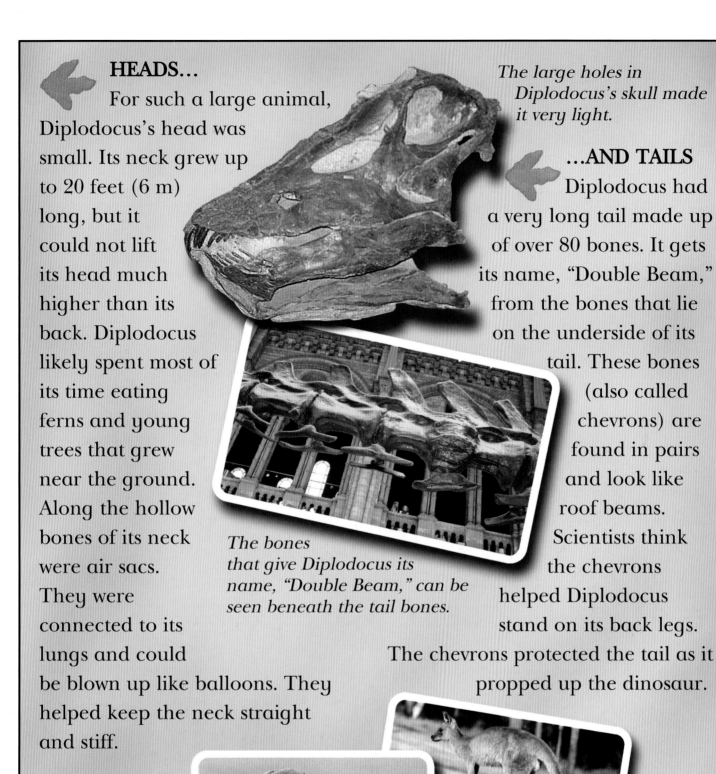

The bones that give Diplodocus its name, "Double Beam," can be seen beneath the tail bones.

Diplodocus had the long neck of a giraffe, the huge body and strong legs of an elephant, and, to balance its neck, the tail of a kangaroo.

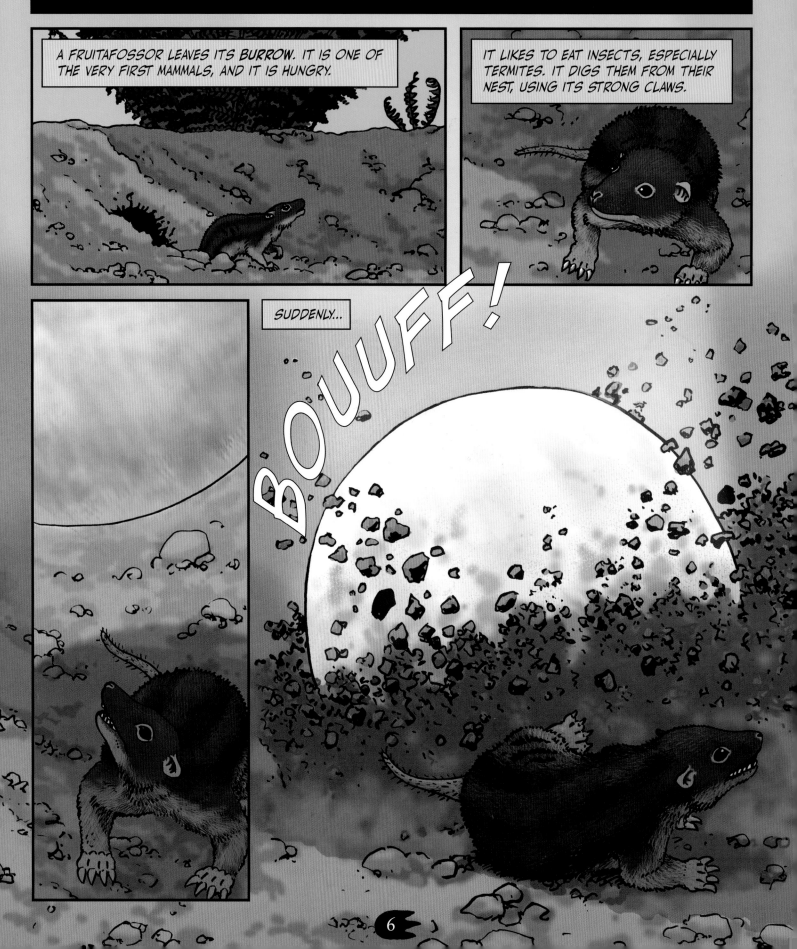

...TOWERING ABOVE THE TINY MAMMAL, A DIPLODOCUS IS LAYING ITS EGGS.

IT IS ONE OF A HERD OF DIPLODOCUSES. EACH YEAR THEY ARRIVE, AND LAY THEIR EGGS. WHEN ALL THEIR EGGS HAVE BEEN LAID, THEY LEAVE. THEY DO NOT WAIT FOR THE EGGS TO HATCH.

A YOUNG DIPLODOCUS WATCHES THE ADULTS. SHE IS TOO SMALL TO BE A HERD MEMBER, THOUGH. SHE HAS SPENT THE LAST THREE YEARS SINCE SHE HATCHED AT THE NESTING SITE. ONE DAY, WHEN SHE IS BIGGER, SHE WILL LEAVE WITH THE HERD.

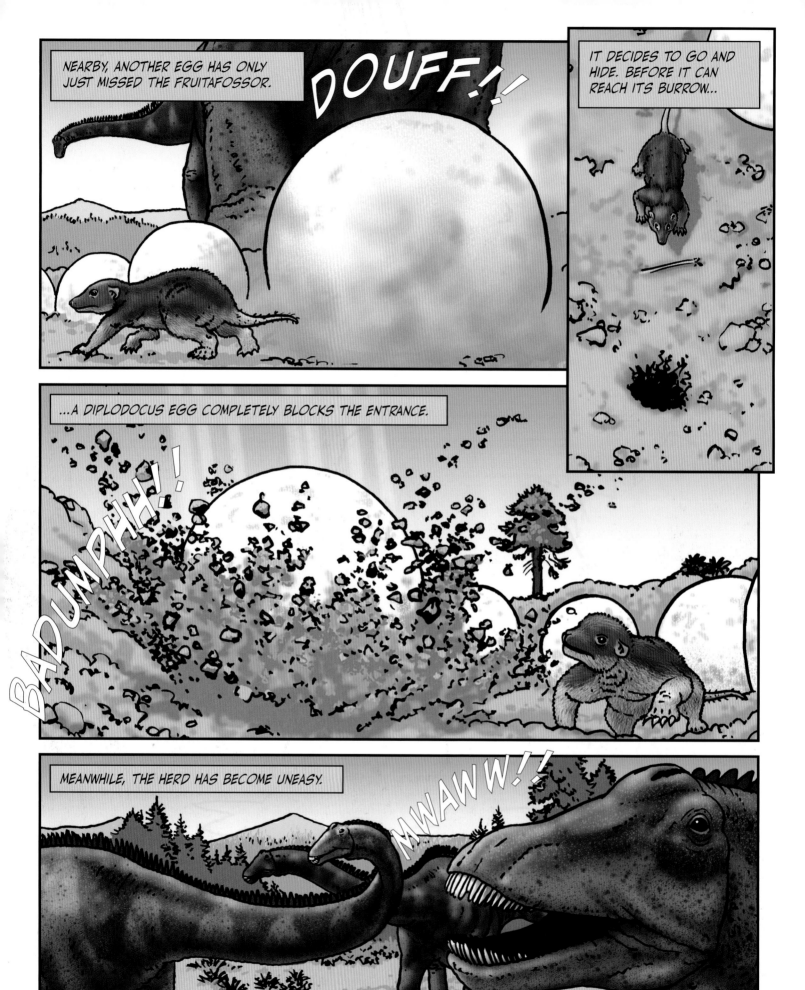

A PAIR OF STEGOSAURUSES HAVE WANDERED INTO THE NESTING SITE. IF THEY DO NOT GO AWAY, THEY MIGHT DESTROY THE EGGS.

THE ADULT DIPLODOCUSES TRY TO SCARE THE STEGOSAURUSES AWAY.

MWAWW!!

OUARRR!!

BROAWW!!

BUT THE STEGOSAURUSES STAY WHERE THEY ARE. THEY SPIN AROUND AND TRY TO HIT THE DIPLODOCUSES WITH THEIR SPIKED TAILS.

A DIPLODOCUS REARS UP ON ITS BACK LEGS TO DODGE THE SPIKES.

IT CRASHES BACK DOWN TO THE GROUND AND ALMOST CRUSHES A STEGOSAURUS.

KERUMPP!!!

RARRKK!!!

THE STEGOSAURUSES HAVE LOST THEIR FIGHT WITH THE DIPLODOCUSES. THEY TURN AND RUN...

...INTO THE PATH OF THE YOUNG DIPLODOCUS...

...WHO IS DESPERATE TO GET OUT OF THEIR WAY...

...BEFORE SHE IS TRAMPLED.

ARRRKK!!

THE FRUITAFOSSOR HAS NOT NOTICED THE FIGHT. IT IS BUSY TRYING TO MOVE THE EGG THAT IS BLOCKING THE OPENING TO ITS BURROW.

ALL THREE DINOSAURS BOLT THROUGH THE NESTING SITE.

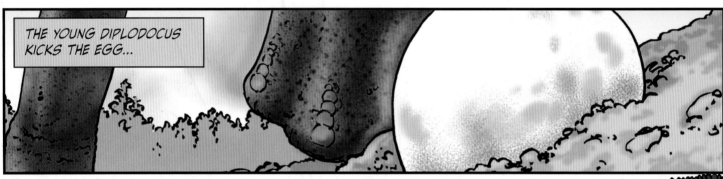

THE YOUNG DIPLODOCUS KICKS THE EGG...

...AND SENDS IT FLYING ACROSS THE GROUND.

DUMPHH!

THE ENTRANCE TO THE BURROW IS OPEN AGAIN. INSIDE IS THE FRUITAFOSSOR'S FAMILY. THE YOUNG DIPLODOCUS HAS SET THEM FREE.

THE TWO STEGOSAURUSES WANDER AWAY FROM THE NESTS. BEHIND THEM THE YOUNG DIPLODOCUS IS UNHARMED AND THE DIPLODOCUS EGGS ARE UNBROKEN.

IT IS A FEW DAYS LATER AND THE NESTING SEASON IS OVER FOR ANOTHER YEAR. THE DIPLODOCUS HERD MOVES ON TO FIND NEW FEEDING GROUNDS. THE YOUNG DIPLODOCUS IS NOT YET BIG ENOUGH TO GO WITH THEM. MAYBE IT WILL BE HER TURN NEXT YEAR.

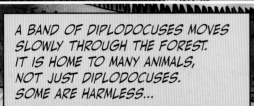

PART TWO... NEIGHBORS

A BAND OF DIPLODOCUSES MOVES SLOWLY THROUGH THE FOREST. IT IS HOME TO MANY ANIMALS, NOT JUST DIPLODOCUSES. SOME ARE HARMLESS...

...OTHERS ARE NOT.

THE CHARGE BY THE ORNITHOLESTES IS SUDDEN...

EEEAWWKK!!

...AND SUCCESSFUL. IT HAS CAUGHT A ONE-YEAR-OLD DIPLODOCUS HATCHLING.

THE YOUNG DIPLODOCUS HAS SEEN THE ATTACK. THE MEAT EATER DOES NOT SCARE HER, THOUGH.

SHE IS FOUR YEARS OLD AND HAS GROWN TOO LARGE TO BE THREATENED BY AN ORNITHOLESTES.

A PAIR OF GARGOYLEOSAURUSES WANDER PAST, BROWSING ON FERNS AS THEY GO.

THEY ROAR AND HISS AT THE DIPLODOCUS, WARNING HER TO KEEP AWAY. THEY ARE NOT MEAT EATERS, BUT THEY WILL SLASH AT THE DIPLODOCUS WITH THEIR ARMORED TAILS IF SHE GETS TOO CLOSE.

BRAWWKK!!

THE YOUNG DIPLODOCUS COMES TO A FOREST CLEARING.

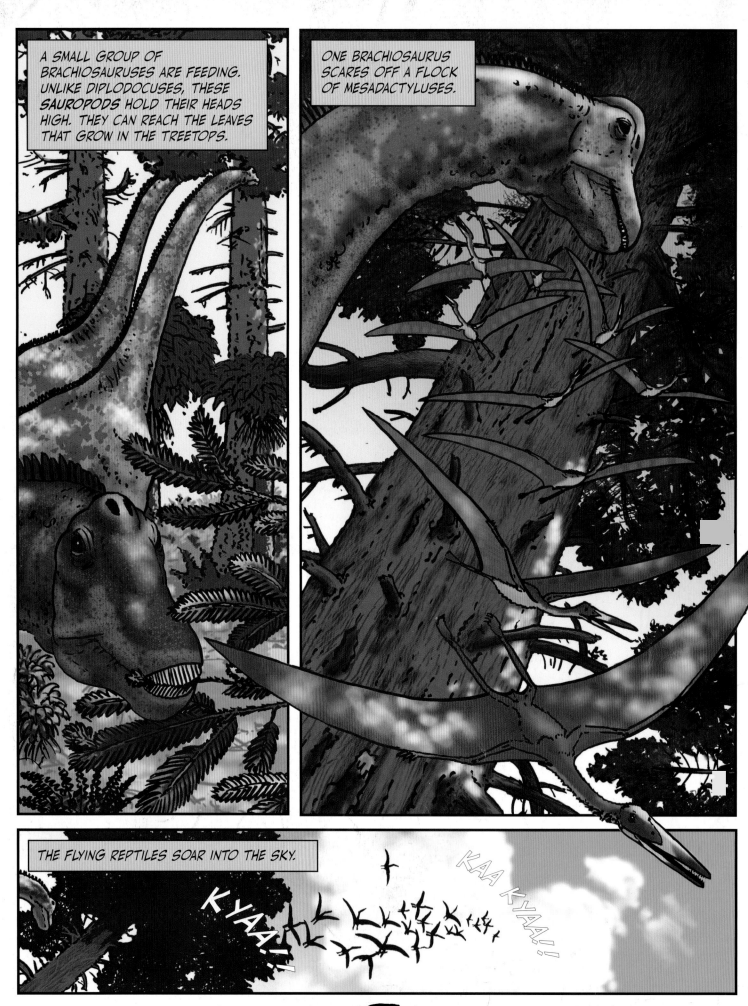

A SMALL GROUP OF BRACHIOSAURUSES ARE FEEDING. UNLIKE DIPLODOCUSES, THESE **SAUROPODS** HOLD THEIR HEADS HIGH. THEY CAN REACH THE LEAVES THAT GROW IN THE TREETOPS.

ONE BRACHIOSAURUS SCARES OFF A FLOCK OF MESADACTYLUSES.

THE FLYING REPTILES SOAR INTO THE SKY.

KYAA!

KAA KYAA!

SOME OF THE MESADACTYLUSES FLY TOWARD THE RIVER TO CATCH FISH.

OTHERS SWOOP INTO THE FOREST...

...TO HUNT DRAGONFLIES.

17

THE YOUNG DIPLODOCUS WALKS BACK INTO THE FOREST.

WITHOUT WARNING, A GROUP OF DRYOSAURUSES DART FROM THE SHADOWS, STARTLING THE DIPLODOCUS. SOMETHING HAS SCARED THEM.

ARRKK!!

WARRKK!

THERE ARE LARGER, MORE DANGEROUS DINOSAURS IN THE FOREST THAN ORNITHOLESTESES. THE DIPLODOCUS HIDES...

...JUST IN TIME. A CERATOSAURUS PASSES NEAR HER. THE LARGE MEAT EATER IS CHASING THE DRYOSAURUSES AND DOES NOT NOTICE THE HIDING DIPLODOCUS.

SUDDENLY THE PLANTS NEXT TO HER BEGIN TO SHAKE. HAS THE CERATOSAURUS RETURNED?

RUSTLE

RUSTLE

AN ADULT DIPLODOCUS POKES ITS HEAD BETWEEN THE TREES TO REACH THE TENDER FERNS.

THE DIPLODOCUS HERD HAS ARRIVED.

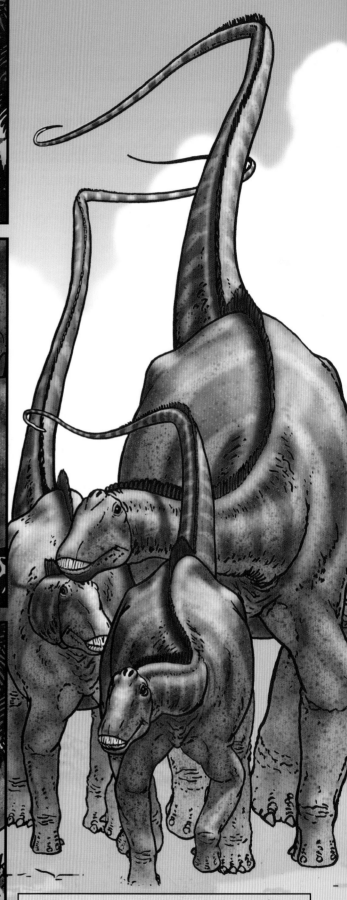

THIS YEAR WHEN THE HERD LEAVES THE NESTING SITE, THE YOUNG DIPLODOCUS GOES WITH THEM.

PART THREE

THE FOG

THE HERD HAS WANDERED DOWN TO A SMALL LAKE TO DRINK. A FOG HAS SETTLED OVER THE WATER, AND THE YOUNG DIPLODOCUS IS LOST. SHE CALLS OUT AND THE HERD ANSWERS.

BUT, IN THE FOG, THEIR CRIES SEEM TO COME FROM ALL AROUND HER. SHE DOES NOT KNOW WHICH WAY TO GO.

SHE SEES A SHAPE. IT COULD BE ANOTHER HERD MEMBER.

IT IS ONLY THE BONES OF A BRACHIOSAURUS.

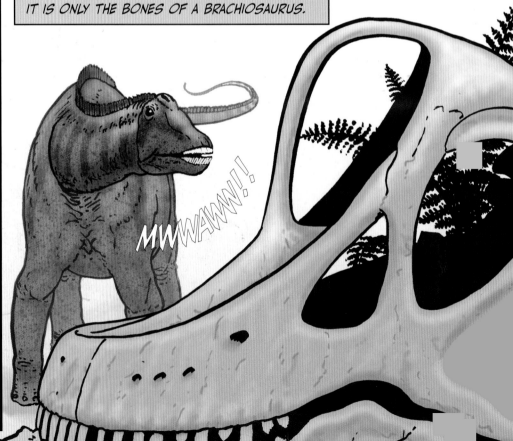

SHE MOVES ON. IT HAS BEEN LESS THAN A YEAR SINCE THE DIPLODOCUS LEFT THE NESTING GROUNDS AND JOINED THE HERD.

SHE HAS GROWN IN THAT TIME, BUT STILL NEEDS THE LARGE ADULTS TO PROTECT HER. SHE FEELS SCARED WHEN THEY ARE NOT NEARBY.

MWWWAWW!!

A NOISE STARTLES THE YOUNG DIPLODOCUS.

SOMETHING IS COMING.

PLOOSHH!

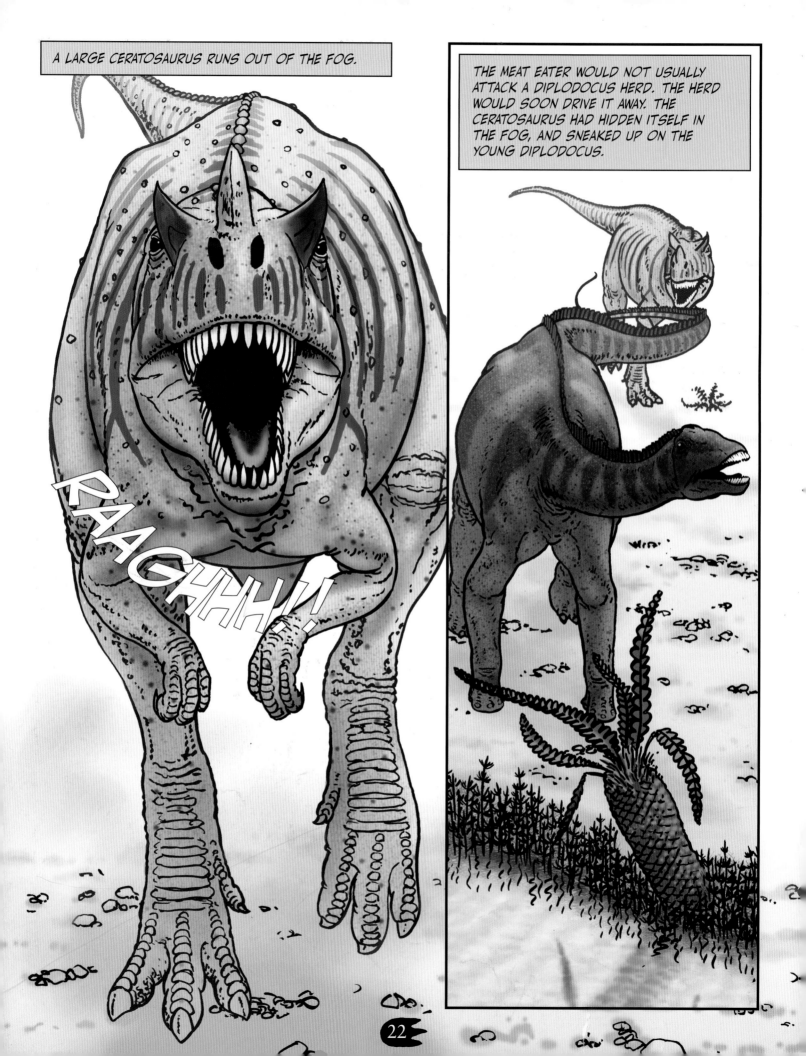

A LARGE CERATOSAURUS RUNS OUT OF THE FOG.

THE MEAT EATER WOULD NOT USUALLY ATTACK A DIPLODOCUS HERD. THE HERD WOULD SOON DRIVE IT AWAY. THE CERATOSAURUS HAD HIDDEN ITSELF IN THE FOG, AND SNEAKED UP ON THE YOUNG DIPLODOCUS.

RAAGHHH!!!

THE DIPLODOCUS RUNS BACK TOWARD THE BRACHIOSAURUS BONES.

SHE IS NOT A FAST RUNNER. WITH EVERY STRIDE, THE CERATOSAURUS GETS CLOSER...

...AND CLOSER.

THE DIPLODOCUS STOPS RUNNING. THE MEAT EATER IS NO LONGER CHASING HER.

A BREEZE STARTS TO BLOW THE FOG AWAY.

ALL AROUND HER ARE MEMBERS OF THE HERD. SHE IS SAFE AGAIN.

PART FOUR

THE TRAP

THE HERD IS UNDER ATTACK! THE ADULT DIPLODOCUSES SNAP THEIR TAILS AT TWO ALLOSAURUSES. THE BOOMING SOUND THE TAILS MAKE SCARES THE MEAT EATERS. THE DIPLODOCUS ADULTS ARE CAREFUL TO KEEP THEMSELVES BETWEEN THE ALLOSAURUSES AND THE SMALL JUVENILES.

KERRACK!!

THE ALLOSAURUSES HAVE A PLAN. TWO MORE PACK MEMBERS ATTACK THE HERD FROM BEHIND.

WITH THE ADULTS BUSY, THEY MIGHT BE ABLE TO BRING DOWN A WEAKER JUVENILE.

MEANWHILE, THE YOUNG DIPLODOCUS STAYS CLOSE TO THE ADULTS. SHE HAS BEEN WITH THE HERD FOR OVER A YEAR, BUT SHE IS STILL TOO SMALL TO DEFEND HERSELF AGAINST A FULL-GROWN ALLOSAURUS.

IN THEIR RUSH TO REACH THE DIPLODOCUSES, THE ALLOSAURUSES SURPRISE A HERD OF CAMPTOSAURUSES.

WARRKK!!

THEY RUN TOWARD THE DIPLODOCUSES IN A BLIND PANIC.

THE CAMPTOSAURUSES AND ALLOSAURUSES DART THROUGH THE DIPLODOCUS HERD.

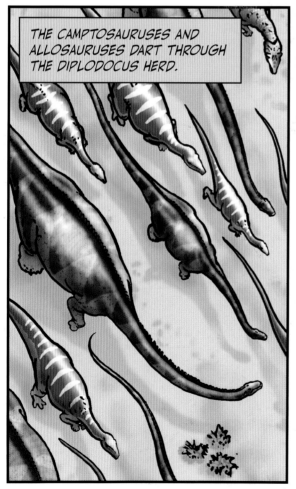

THE YOUNG DIPLODOCUS IS ALARMED AND BEGINS TO RUN WITH THE CAMPTOSAURUSES.

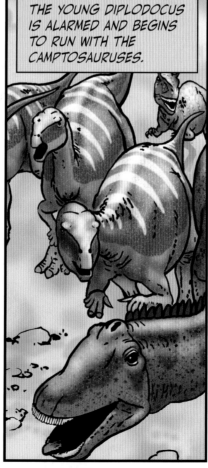

IN THE CONFUSION, ONE OF THE ALLOSAURUSES SEES A CHANCE TO ATTACK.

THE ALLOSAURUS STRIKES. ITS VICTIM IS A CAMPTOSAURUS, NOT THE YOUNG DIPLODOCUS.

WARRKK!!

THE FORCE OF THE ALLOSAURUS'S ATTACK KNOCKS THE TWO DINOSAURS INTO A SMALL, SHALLOW POOL.

BDOOSH!!

THE ALLOSAURUS QUICKLY KILLS THE CAMPTOSAURUS AND STARTS TO FEED. HOWEVER, THE POOL IS DEEPER THAN IT SEEMS.

THE SECOND ALLOSAURUS SPOTS THE YOUNG DIPLODOCUS AND SPRINTS AFTER HER. IT WILL CATCH HER IN JUST A FEW STRIDES.

THE ALLOSAURUS SUDDENLY STOPS.

IT HAS SEEN ITS PACK MATE IN THE POOL WITH THE DEAD CAMPTOSAURUS.

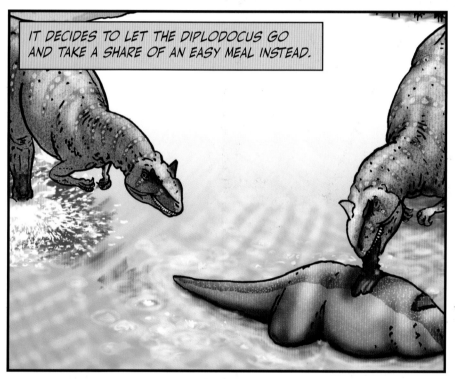

IT DECIDES TO LET THE DIPLODOCUS GO AND TAKE A SHARE OF AN EASY MEAL INSTEAD.

THERE IS THICK, STICKY MUD BENEATH THE POOL'S CLEAR SURFACE. THE CLOSER THE ALLOSAURUS GETS TO ITS MEAL, THE DEEPER IT SINKS.

THE TWO ALLOSAURUSES ARE BEING SLOWLY SUCKED DOWN INTO THE MUDDY POOL. THEY WILL NOT ESCAPE FROM THE STICKY NATURAL TRAP. NEARBY, THE DIPLODOCUS HERD MOVES ON. IT HAS SCARED OFF THE ALLOSAURUSES AND CONTINUES ITS NEVER-ENDING SEARCH FOR FOOD.

FOSSIL EVIDENCE

ALMOST EVERYTHING WE KNOW ABOUT DINOSAURS COMES FROM THEIR FOSSIL REMAINS. FOSSILS FORM WHEN PARTS OF AN ANIMAL OR PLANT ARE BURIED AND TURN TO ROCK OVER A LONG TIME. SCIENTISTS WHO STUDY FOSSILS ARE CALLED PALEONTOLOGISTS.

Fossilized bones are not the only fossils that give us clues about how dinosaurs lived. Sometimes fossil footprints are found. Tracks made by sauropods, such as Diplodocuses, show that they moved from place to place in herds. Juveniles walked in the center, protected by the adults at the outside. Titanosaurs, another group of sauropods, laid their eggs in huge nesting sites. Diplodocus herds may have laid their eggs in the same way. Sauropod eggs were large. The fossil sauropod egg shown below is 12 inches (30 cm) long and 10 inches (25 cm) wide. They were strong as well. When it was laid, an egg would have dropped at least 8 feet (2.5 m) to the ground.

ANIMAL GALLERY

Mesadactylus
"Mesa finger"
Wingspan: 3 ft (1 m)
A small flying reptile that ate fish, lizards, and insects.

Ornitholestes
"Bird robber"
Length: 6 ft (2 m)
A small, fast-moving meat eater.

Dryosaurus
"Oak lizard"
Length: 12 ft (3.5 m)
A plant eater that was called "Oak lizard" because its cheek teeth look like tiny oak leaves.

Ceratosaurus
"Horned lizard"
Length: 20–26 ft (6–8 m)
A meat eater that may have been a good swimmer.

Stegosaurus
"Roof lizard"
Length: 30 ft (9 m)
A dinosaur that may have used the plates on its back to help control its temperature.

Gargoyleosaurus
"Gargoyle lizard"
Length: 13 ft (4 m)
A fairly small dinosaur with armor that made it weigh over 1 ton (907 kg).

Camptosaurus
"Bent lizard"
Length: 26 ft (8 m)
A plant eater that could walk and run on either two or four legs.

Brachiosaurus
"Arm lizard"
Length: 82 ft (25 m)
A sauropod that could lift its head 42 feet (13 m) above the ground.

Allosaurus
"Different lizard"
Length: 28 ft (8.5 m)
A meat eater that was the top predator of its day and may have hunted in packs.

GLOSSARY

browsing (BROWZ-ing) Feeding on grass or leaves by nibbling here and there.

burrow (BUR-oh) A small animal's home dug out of the ground.

desperate (DES-puh-rit) Feeling as if one has no hope.

fossils (FO-sulz) The remains of living things that have turned to rock.

Jurassic period (ju-RA-sik PIR-ee-ud) The time between 200 million years ago and 145 million years ago.

juveniles (JOO-vuh-nylz) Young animals that are not fully grown.

sauropods (SOR-uh-podz) Large four-footed, plant-eating dinosaurs with long necks and tails and small heads.

site (SYT) The place where a certain event happens.

INDEX

Web Sites
Due to the changing nature of Internet links, the Rosen Publishing Group, Inc., has developed an online list of Web sites related to the subject of this book. This site is updated regularly. Please use this link to access the list:
www.powerkidslinks.com/gdino/diplo/